Walter, Now they'll have to
show the
of the

Love,
Connie

Walter, Now they'll have to
show the
of the

WHERE'S BIN LADEN?

ILLUSTRATIONS
DANIEL LALIC

TEXT DEVELOPMENT
XAVIER WATERKEYN

ACKNOWLEDGEMENTS

I'd like to thank my parents for paying my bills all these years, a big thank-you to Fiona Schultz and the New Holland team for giving me a fantastic brief, my friends Lisa Iorfino and Chad Drake for helping me make my deadline, and to my agents, Clare Calvet and Xavier Waterkeyn of Flying Pigs for all their hard work. Thanks, X, we make a great creative team.

Daniel Lalic

TOP SECRET

Agent, we all know that Osama Bin Laden (or 'Bin Baby' to his friends) became super famous after he exploded onto the scene in New York a few years back, but since then we haven't heard much from the man that everybody loves to hate. The burning question of international security is: Where is he and what will be his next greatest hit? Now since the CIA, Interpol, the National Security Agency and the Defense Intelligence Agency have spent zillions of dollars and still haven't had any luck so far it's now up to us to find the world's number one most wanted man. Already, one of our other operatives has managed to trace his movements across the globe. Your mission is to locate the Big BL in the following pages. We have also provided extracts from the previous agent's reports for your information. No doubt Bin Baby will continue to plot and plan attacks near or on some of the biggest icons of the decadent Western capitalist lifestyle.

WHAT TO LOOK FOR

Pictures of all the people and objects mentioned below are on the next page. Look out for them in each location. See also pages 30 and 31 for checklists of other local people and things you may care to find.

BB is getting lots of help from his Posse – his crack Team of Terror. Their names are Loopy, Crazy, Nutty, Freaky, Weirdo, Boom-Boom and Eric. Also tagging along are three wannabe suicide bombers the Bin Ladketeers. Their names are not important.

Obsessive NSA Agent Jimmy Dorch desperately needs a promotion and pay rise to fund for his increasingly expensive 'habits', terrorist groupie Patty Furst wants to have Osama's baby to get back at her parents for neglecting her during her 'Sensitive Years,' and Moonie, the International Exhibitionist, is in every scene purely to provide gratuitous nudity.

Bin Baby may be getting careless. In each scene look for his machine gun, scimitar, hand grenade, bundle of dynamite, mine, stolen CIA Handbook and a UN Map for Installations of Mass Destruction.

Good luck. Agent, the future of the free world depends on you.

Osama Bin Laden

The Posse:
Loopy Crazy Nutty Freaky Weirdo Boom-Boom Eric

Bin Ladketeers

NSA Agent
Jimmy Dorch

Patty Furst

Moonie

Machine Gun

Scimitar

Hand Grenade Bundle of Dynamite Land mine

CIA Handbook

UN Map for Installations
of Mass Destruction

PARIS

Bin Baby's World Tour of Mayhem begins
with yet *another* tower ...

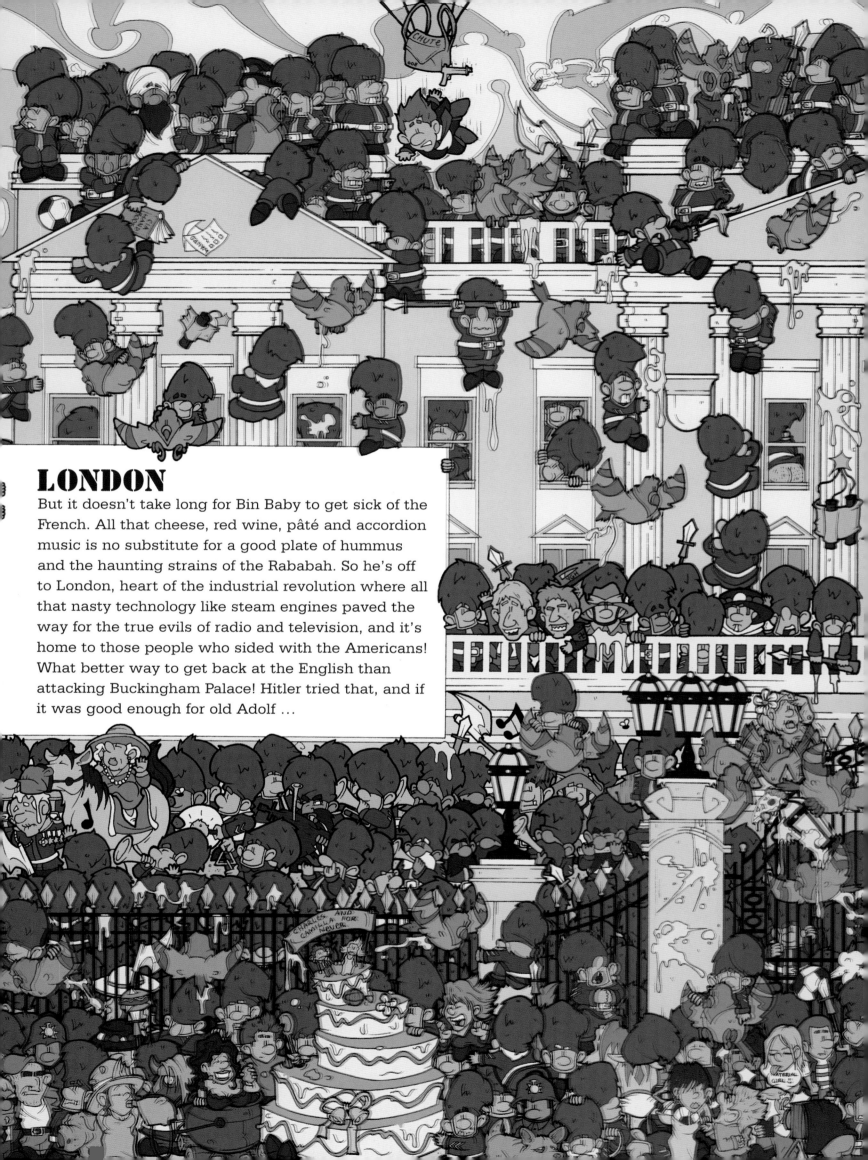

LONDON

But it doesn't take long for Bin Baby to get sick of the French. All that cheese, red wine, pâté and accordion music is no substitute for a good plate of hummus and the haunting strains of the Rababah. So he's off to London, heart of the industrial revolution where all that nasty technology like steam engines paved the way for the true evils of radio and television, and it's home to those people who sided with the Americans! What better way to get back at the English than attacking Buckingham Palace! Hitler tried that, and if it was good enough for old Adolf …

SPAIN

If there's anything than Bin Baby can't stand, it's the idea of Westerners having a good time. One of the few events that BB approves of though is the Bull Run in Pamplona. Part of the Festival of San Fermin, the Run takes place every morning between July 7 and July 14. It's three minutes of jam-packed action with a strong chance that several tourists could get injured and die in an urban cattle stampede. No wonder Bin Baby likes it! Especially when, with a little help from him, there could even be more blood and gore than usual …

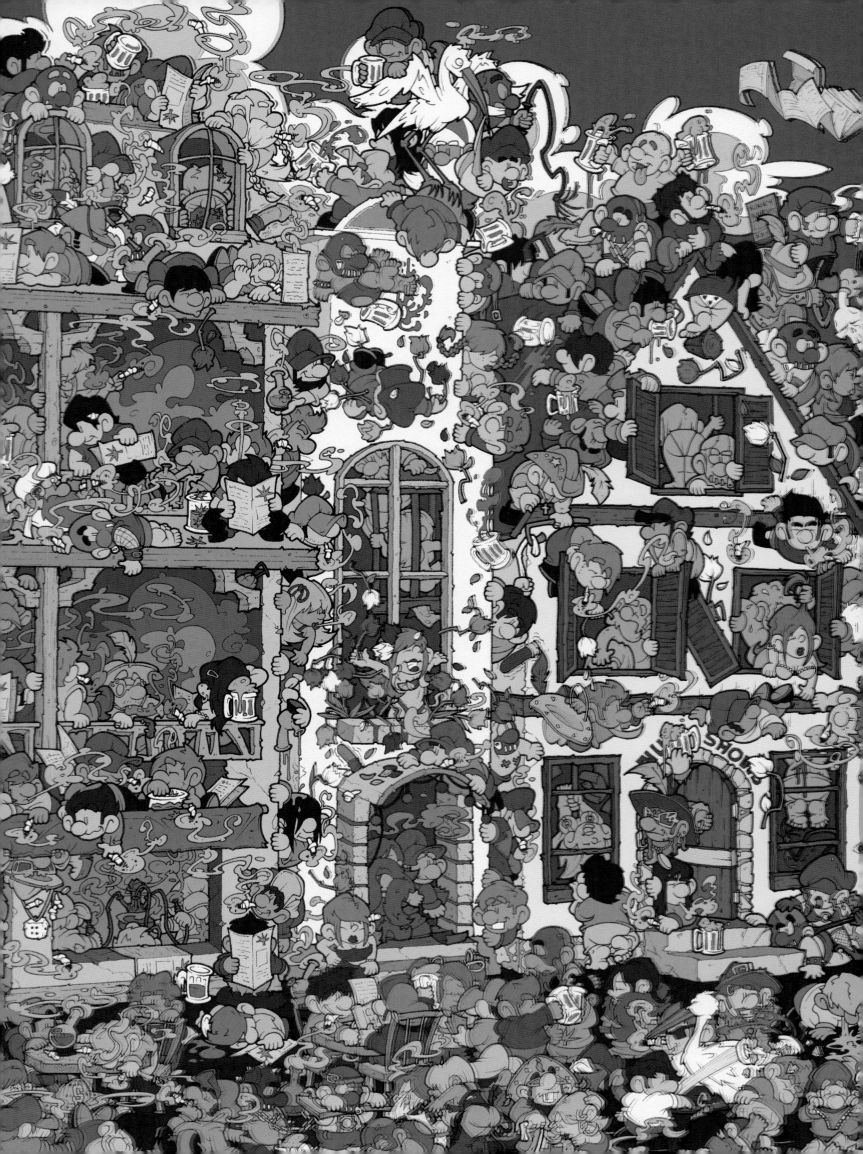

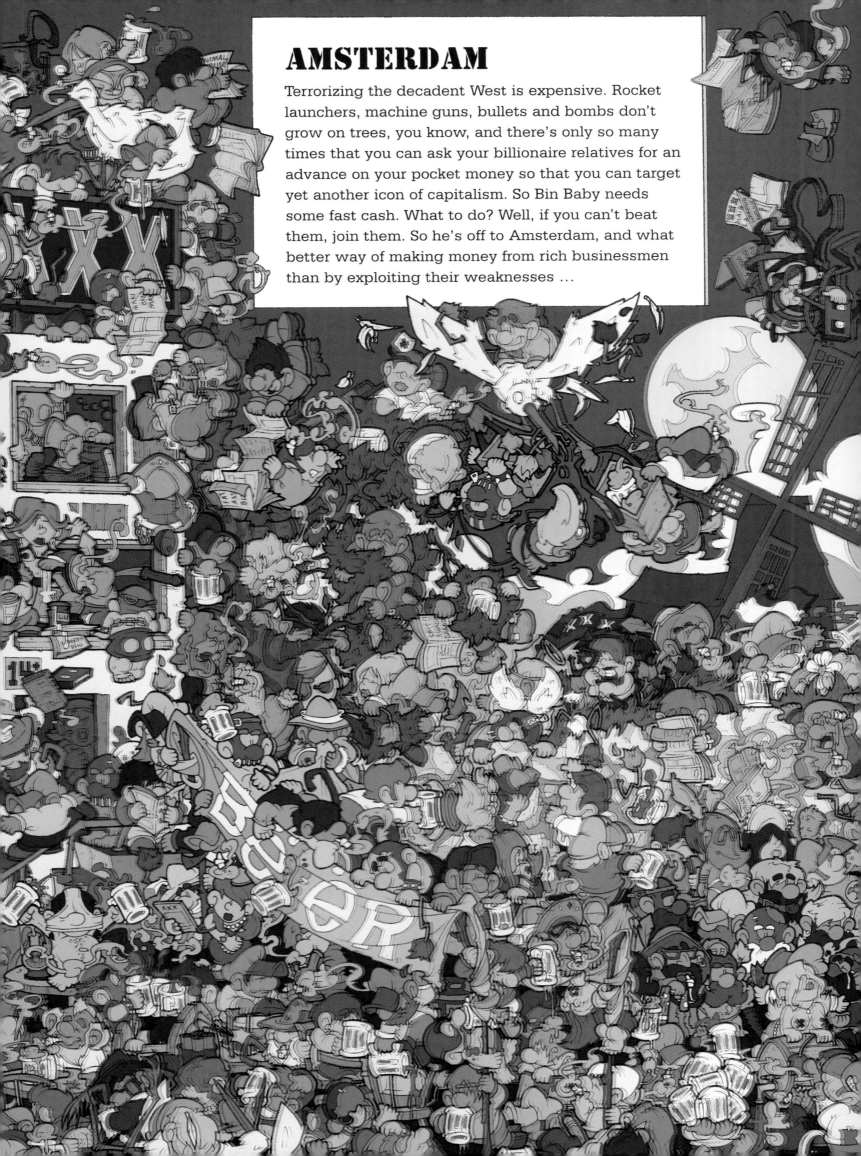

AMSTERDAM

Terrorizing the decadent West is expensive. Rocket launchers, machine guns, bullets and bombs don't grow on trees, you know, and there's only so many times that you can ask your billionaire relatives for an advance on your pocket money so that you can target yet another icon of capitalism. So Bin Baby needs some fast cash. What to do? Well, if you can't beat them, join them. So he's off to Amsterdam, and what better way of making money from rich businessmen than by exploiting their weaknesses …

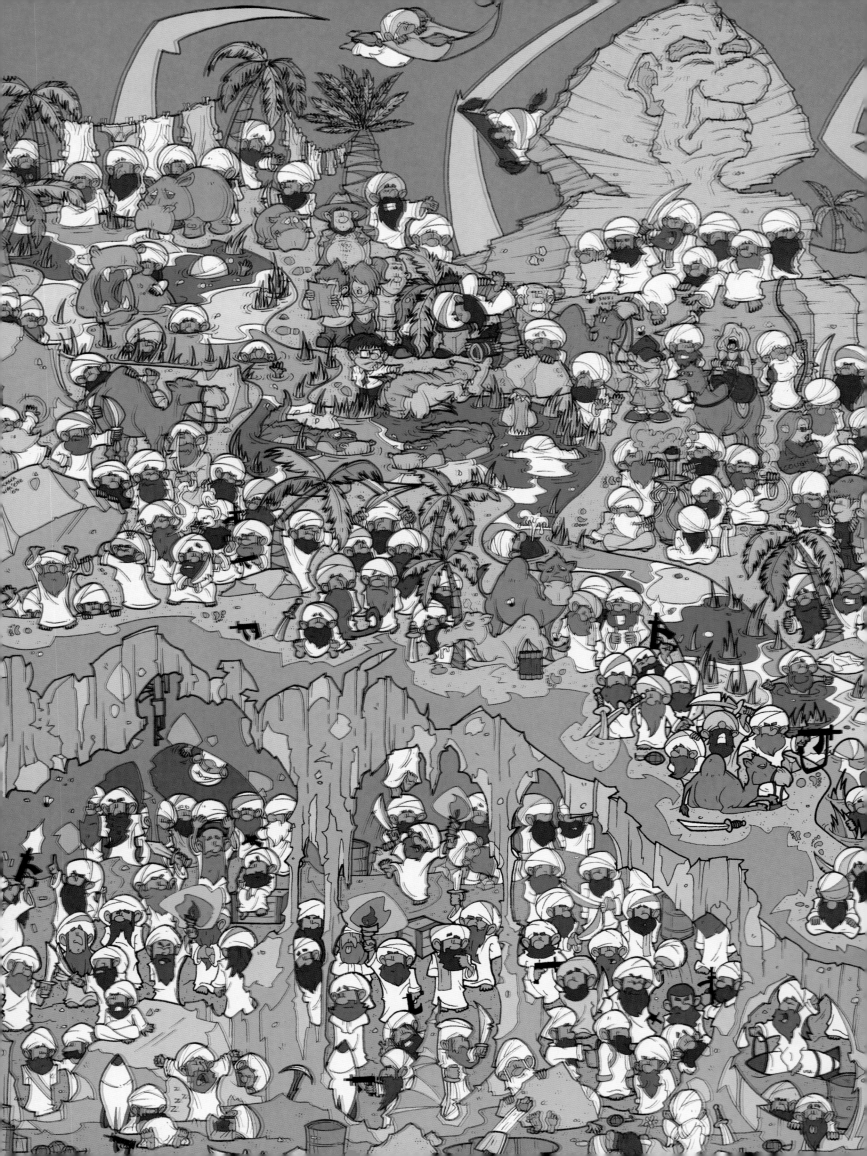

CAIRO

Flush with cash from a few nights of hard labor and soft mattresses Bin Baby and his Posse are now ready to go on a shopping spree. But first, they have to find their way through the markets and tourists of Cairo to find the Secret Underground Arms Trade Fair where there are bargains to be had galore. And you can get two atom bombs for the price of three …

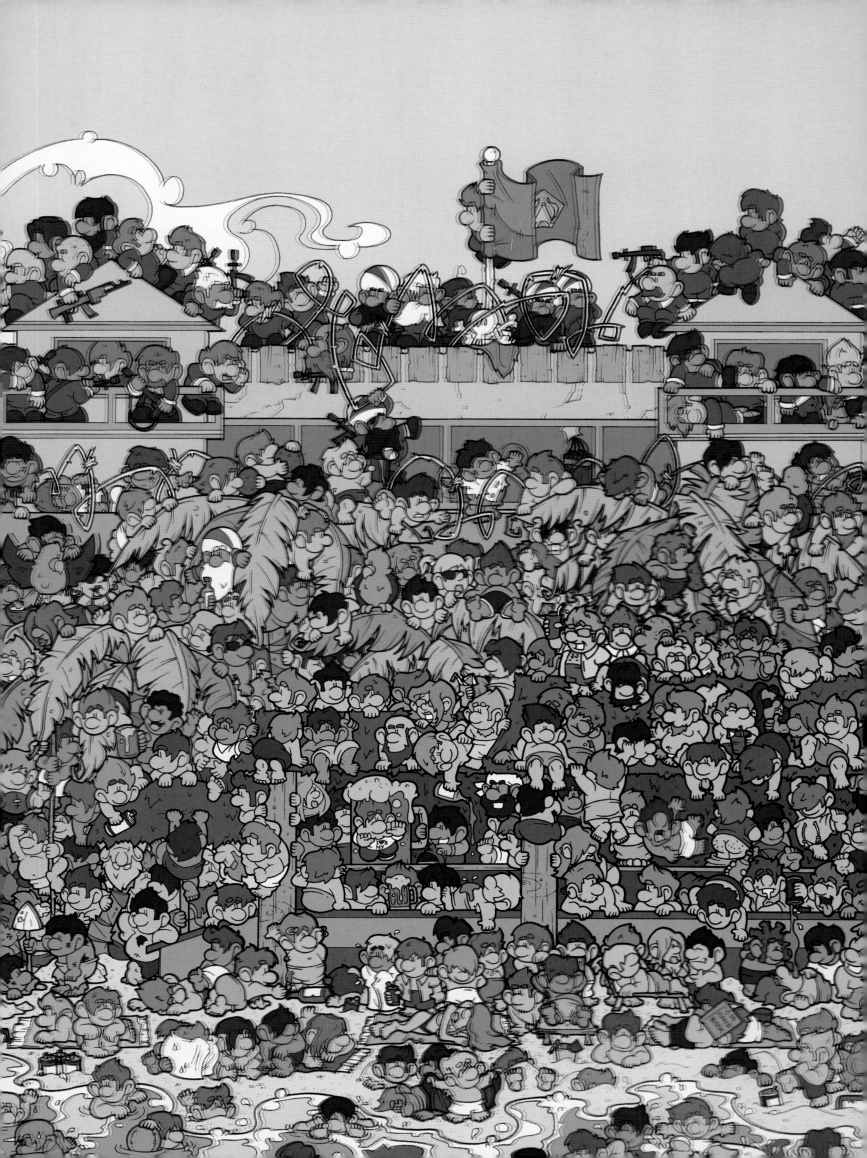

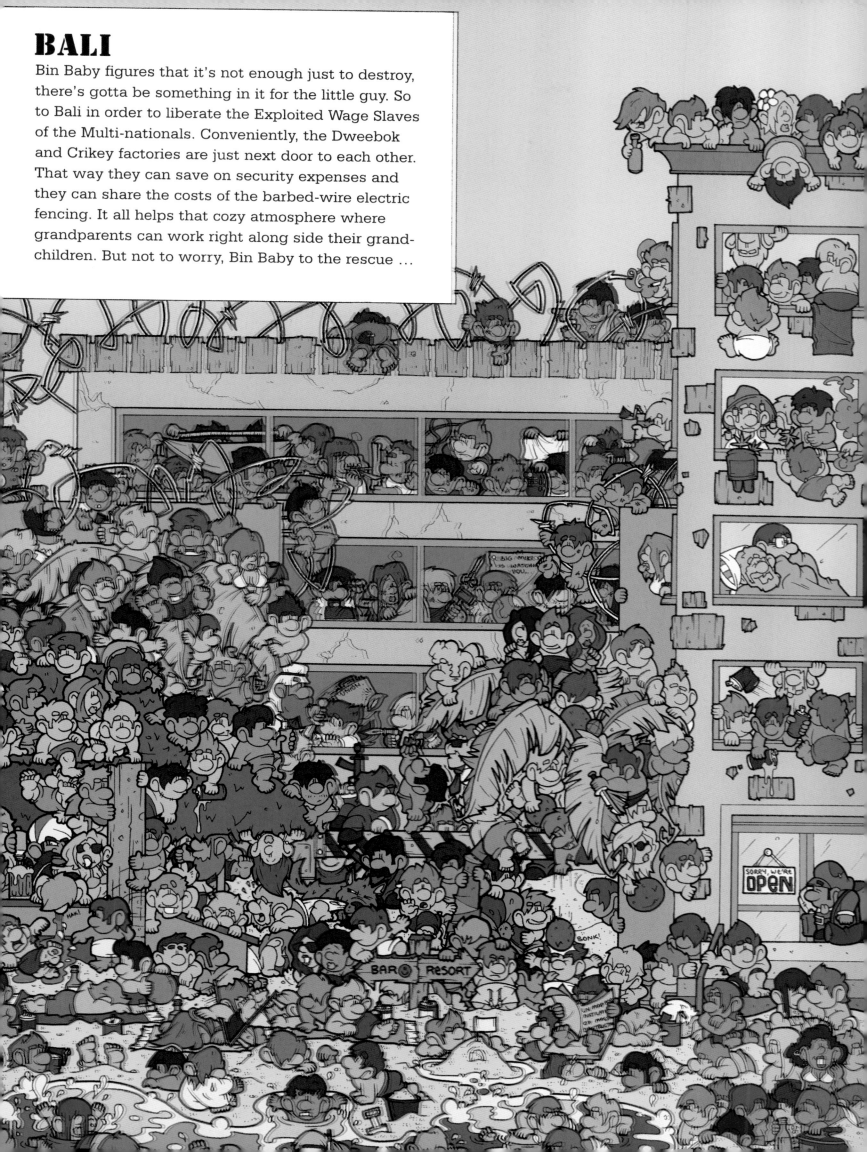

BALI

Bin Baby figures that it's not enough just to destroy, there's gotta be something in it for the little guy. So to Bali in order to liberate the Exploited Wage Slaves of the Multi-nationals. Conveniently, the Dweebok and Crikey factories are just next door to each other. That way they can save on security expenses and they can share the costs of the barbed-wire electric fencing. It all helps that cozy atmosphere where grandparents can work right along side their grand-children. But not to worry, Bin Baby to the rescue …

HONG KONG

Hong Kong and it's already Chinese New Year. How time and fireworks fly when you're having fun! If there's anything worse that Westerners enjoying themselves, it's Easterners enjoying themselves. So, while he's still in Asia, the O Man might as well create a little havoc. Bin Baby loves a good bang, and Hong Kong is just full of them …

SYDNEY

Now normally a high-profile terrorist like the Big O wouldn't be interested in Australia. (It's a looooong way from anywhere else). About the only thing it's got going for it is that there's a lot of desert. But when Australia joined the Axis of Freedom to get back at BL by attacking Iraq well … It's all too confusing really, but still to attack Sydney with its smug-looking Opera House and Bridge? BL figures Hijra could build a better bridge with one hand cut off. Maybe they could get the rebuilding contract? Why should the Carlyle Group be the only ones to make a profit out of terrorism?

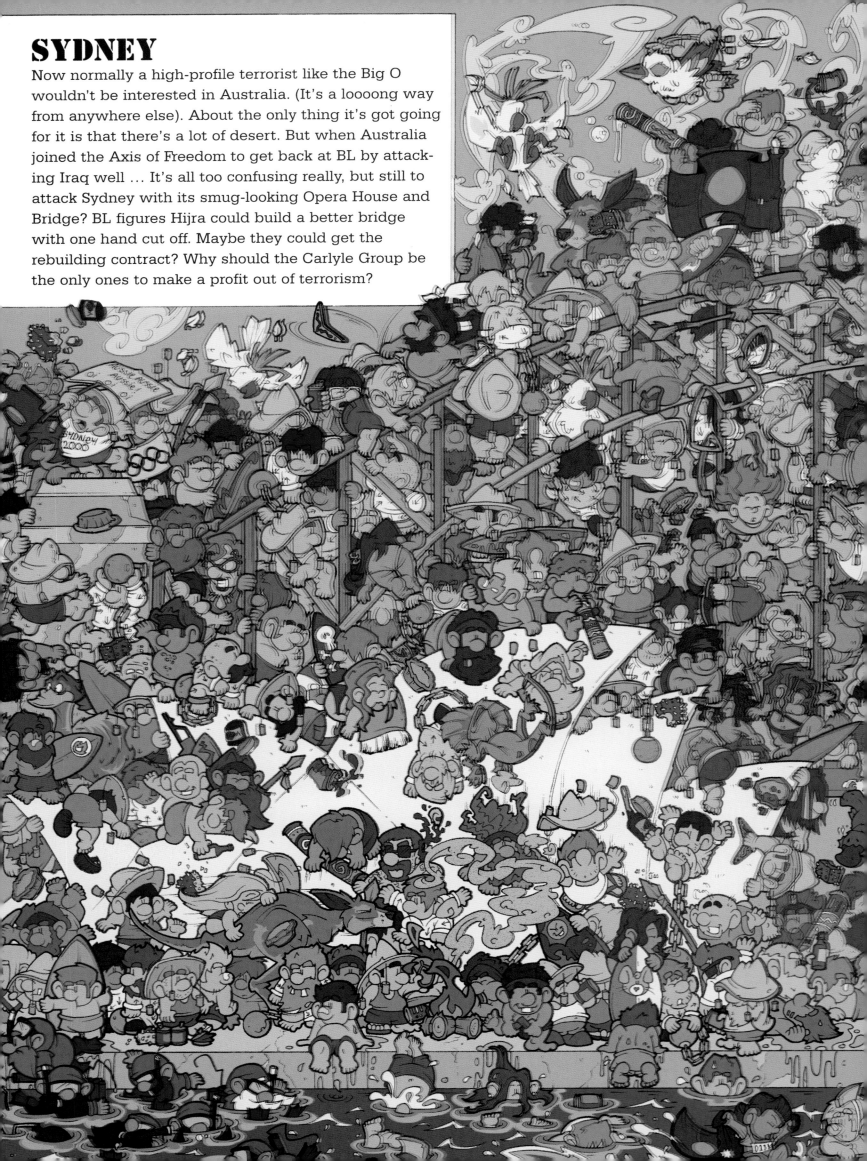

CALIFORNIA

It's no real fun annoying Australians. All they ever end up saying is "She'll be right" before they start another barbecue. If you're serious about getting at Westerners you need to go to the USA. And where better to start than in the West of the West in a place where the kiddies are amusing themselves. Children are, after all, legitimate targets—the child of today is the enemy of tomorrow and if you want to find children training to be the consumers of the future you need to go to Dizzyland …

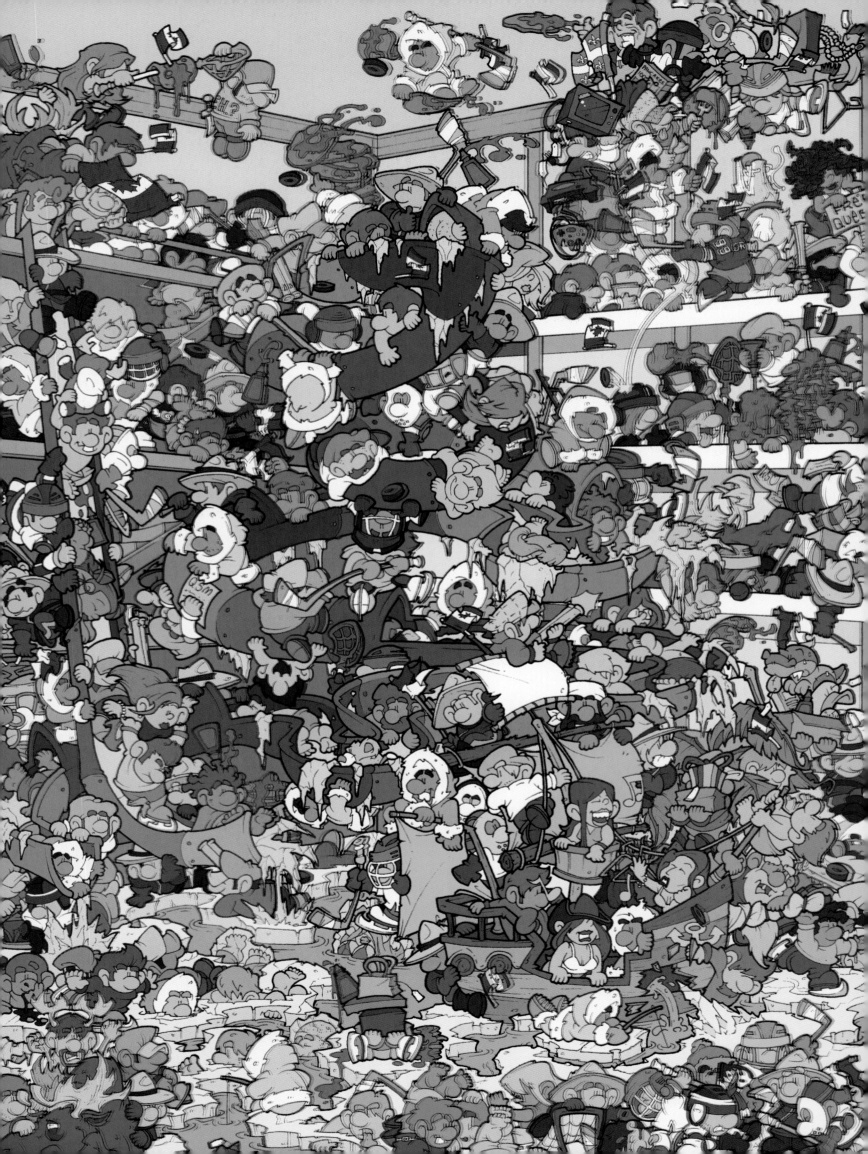

CANADA

Canada, O Canada. In his more philosophical moods Bin Baby likes to argue with himself (no one else would dare!). He asks himself: 'Is the neighbor of my enemy also my enemy?'. After several milliseconds pondering this deep question he answers 'Yes!' Especially when Canada is home to West Edmonton Mall, the worlds biggest shopping complex. What greater symbol of greed and depravity could you ask for? Those shoppers have got it coming to them, alrighty …

NEW YORK

If shopping wasn't offensive enough somebody had to go an make a circus out of it, and Macy's Thanksgiving Day Parade and its worship of capitalist graven and inflatable images is enough to set this fundamentalist boy's blood boiling. It's time to revisit to New York, Osama's home-away-from-home to teach those Yankees another thing or two about true spiritual values …

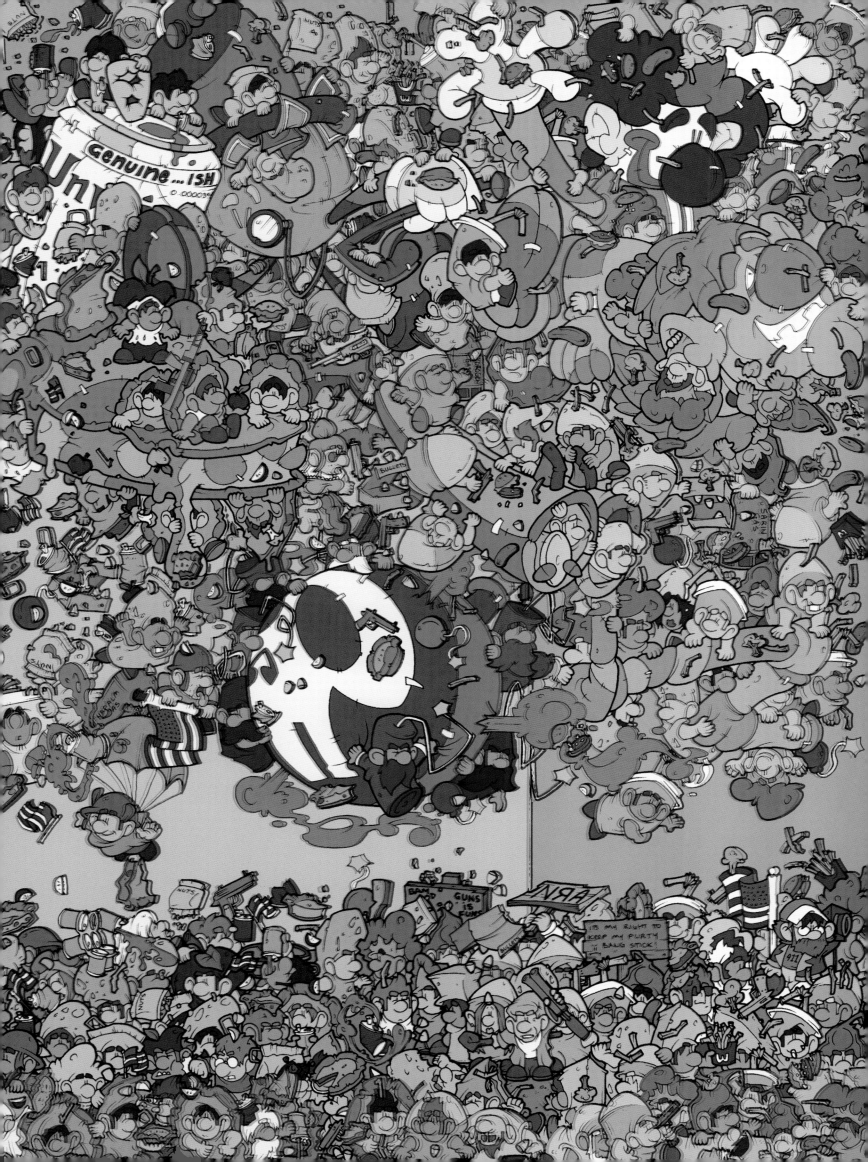

AFGHANIS

It's been a hard year's terrorizing. Time to let your ghutra down, relax put away the explosive the missiles and the barrels of cholera and just take it easy. Let it all hang out and have an end-of-year pajama party at the top secret Al Qa'ida Palace and

CHECK LIST
for further things and people to look for

■ FRANCE – PARIS – EIFFEL TOWER

- ☐ Peasant making wine
- ☐ Gerard Depardieu asking for coins
- ☐ Waiter serving frogs' legs and a snail
- ☐ The Hunchback of Notre Dame
- ☐ Lucy Jordan in a sports car with the warm wind in her hair
- ☐ Parisian riding a giant snail
- ☐ Man hanging on in udder desperation
- ☐ Woman in cheese
- ☐ Man crying from fear of flying
- ☐ Man eating a breadstick
- ☐ Man holding bird egg
- ☐ Man using a plastic bag as a parachute
- ☐ Person trapped in frog
- ☐ Grey and green snails racing
- ☐ An uncomfortable wedgie

■ ENGLAND – LONDON – BUCKINGHAM PALACE

- ☐ Madonna upset over Posh's media attention
- ☐ Kate Moss, Naomi Campbell and Liz Hurley chain smoking
- ☐ Jamie Oliver cooking Nigella Lawson
- ☐ Tony Blair with pigeon poop on his head
- ☐ Two separate extra terrorists providing back-up
- ☐ Hugh Grant paying off another hooker
- ☐ Charles and Camilla
- ☐ Franchised secret agent falling to his death
- ☐ Prince Harry in Nazi uniform
- ☐ Bird flying out of furry hat in magic trick
- ☐ Fergie leaping at food
- ☐ Four separate soccer balls
- ☐ Soldier impaled on fence
- ☐ Poop running down Prince Phillip's face
- ☐ Guard teasing pigeon with a worm

■ SPAIN – PAMPLONA – BULL RUN

- ☐ Bull struggling with horns in barricade
- ☐ Rodeo clown
- ☐ Spaniard throwing trash out the window
- ☐ Man pulling himself together (literally)
- ☐ Matador daring enough to wave red cloth
- ☐ Man clinging to a nose ring
- ☐ Small child tight rope walking
- ☐ Two separate men leap-frogging to safety
- ☐ Spanish flea circus
- ☐ Man escaping the bedroom of his mistress
- ☐ Impaled on a horn stomach first
- ☐ Impaled on a horn spine first
- ☐ Texan riding a mechanical bull
- ☐ A severed leg
- ☐ A bull tagged on the ear

■ NETHERLANDS – AMSTERDAM – RED LIGHT DISTRICT

- ☐ Stoner reading menu upside-down
- ☐ Skull bong
- ☐ Tub of lubricant
- ☐ Man finger plugging leaky dike
- ☐ Bong water spilt on head
- ☐ Pimp with a golden tooth
- ☐ Gimp on a leash
- ☐ Inflatable doll
- ☐ 'Spit, Swallow, Gargle' porn magazine
- ☐ 'F**king Dirty Vol.4' porn tape
- ☐ Gays in bondage kissing
- ☐ Love heart panties
- ☐ Cage dancer
- ☐ Man bathing in a beer keg
- ☐ Anal beads

■ EGYPT – CAIRO – NILE

- ☐ Bin Baby's graffiti
- ☐ Tug of war with facial hair
- ☐ A pair of underwear
- ☐ A flower for the deceased
- ☐ Thief with his hand in a barrel
- ☐ Sniffing feet
- ☐ Man cleaning ear with camel tail
- ☐ Skinny dipper
- ☐ Tour guide translating for tourists
- ☐ Bedouins smoking hookah
- ☐ Wealthy salesman with jewel in turban
- ☐ Man opening fire on a fly
- ☐ Magic lamp
- ☐ Crocodile pursuing tourist with camera
- ☐ Couple being affectionate

■ BALI – BEACH & SWEATSHOPS

- ☐ Factory workers tunneling to freedom
- ☐ Australian marijuana dealer
- ☐ Yankee tourist drowning in beer
- ☐ A wild dog giving a wedgie
- ☐ Man with four piercings
- ☐ Guard sleeping on the job
- ☐ Beverage with green and white umbrella
- ☐ Tourist trapped in collapsible chair
- ☐ A guard encouraging workers with a whip
- ☐ A topless sunbather
- ☐ A factory worker with an injured arm
- ☐ Three separate tropical birds
- ☐ A snorkeling tourist
- ☐ A worker with three arms
- ☐ A man launching a coconut assault

CHINA – HONG KONG – CHINESE NEW YEAR
- [ ] Bird dying of bird flu
- [ ] An elderly man smoking a pipe
- [ ] Three separate bowls full of fluffy white rice
- [ ] SARS decontaminator holding sparkler
- [ ] Man covered in noodles
- [ ] Tsunami victim floating facedown
- [ ] Bad labelling reveals a bomb
- [ ] Dull brown robes patched up at the butt
- [ ] Mongolian breaching the Great Wall
- [ ] Cracked spectacles
- [ ] Four separate candles
- [ ] A white bowl of grain
- [ ] A three-pronged martial arts weapon
- [ ] A split coolie hat
- [ ] A green-tongued bird flu victim

AUSTRALIA – SYDNEY – HARBOR BRIDGE & OPERA HOUSE
- [ ] Crocodile Hunter fighting for his life
- [ ] Serious sunburn victim
- [ ] Killer koala drop bear
- [ ] Kylie Minogue with gay fan base
- [ ] 'Chopper' Read's ear
- [ ] Prime Minister John Howard
- [ ] Olympics fanatic still celebrating
- [ ] Dame Edna
- [ ] Ned Kelly
- [ ] Actor brawling
- [ ] Cathy Freeman defying physics
- [ ] Dingo stealing a baby
- [ ] 'Actress' refusing an autograph
- [ ] Two separate frilled-necked lizards

USA WEST – CALIFORNIA – DIZZZYLAND
- [ ] A weak jester
- [ ] An Oriental woman's $2 'Sucki'
- [ ] A triple scoop ice cream cone
- [ ] Man trapped in a web
- [ ] Face-painted soldier
- [ ] Terrorist dart board
- [ ] Ice cream plopped onto head
- [ ] Three separate toffee apples
- [ ] A single piece of chalk
- [ ] Rigged bottle game
- [ ] Road rage
- [ ] Man tripped down and bound
- [ ] Four separate spanners
- [ ] A piece of cheese
- [ ] A three of diamonds playing card

CANADA – WEST EDMONTON MALL
- [ ] A particularly violent hockey player
- [ ] Tom Green 'mingling' with moose
- [ ] Shania Twain, Celine Dion and Alanis Morissette competing for attention
- [ ] Man who lost his swimming costume
- [ ] Moose drooling
- [ ] Wrestler Bret 'Hitman' Hart making tap out
- [ ] Adam impersonator with maple leaf
- [ ] Pamela Anderson failing lifeguard duties
- [ ] A hunter becomes the hunted
- [ ] Jim Carrey flings pancake
- [ ] Eight separate animal toys
- [ ] Hockey great Wayne Gretzky causing accident
- [ ] Store no.187
- [ ] Avril Lavigne makes her voice heard
- [ ] Quebec separatist sticking pamphlet to slide

USA EAST – NEW YORK – MACY'S DAY PARADE
- [ ] Napalm, sarin, hydrogen, nerve, tear and mustard gas canisters
- [ ] A pale-skinned American Indian
- [ ] Cannibal French-fry
- [ ] President Bush counting profits from investments in the Carlyle Group
- [ ] Bill Gates attacking man in apple costume
- [ ] Michael Moore searching for new victims to parody
- [ ] Two sets of dog tags
- [ ] Pigtailed girls in mushroom cloud costume
- [ ] Pack of cigarettes containing only two cigs
- [ ] 'Unweiser' alcohol enthusiast giving 'rock on' gesture
- [ ] Female American Indian
- [ ] Twelve W(ea)kDonald's burgers
- [ ] Four separate boxes of bullets
- [ ] Nut bag clinging to a cane
- [ ] Charlton Heston parting a sea of people

AFGHANISTAN – AL QA'IDA PAJAMA PARTY
- [ ] Two nightcaps knotted together
- [ ] Toothpaste prank on a sleeping victim
- [ ] Man surfing down a banister on a pillow
- [ ] Man tarred and feathered
- [ ] Teddy bear concealing a blade
- [ ] Man impersonating a ghost
- [ ] Man floating on a gigantic feather
- [ ] Man with blood moustache
- [ ] A pair of bunny slippers
- [ ] A single pink feather
- [ ] Seven separate torches
- [ ] Head of guillotine victim
- [ ] Veiled man boogying with dancers
- [ ] The only two unbroken, unbitten cookies
- [ ] A man hiding in another's beard

THE END — OR IS IT?

First published in Australia in 2009 by
New Holland Publishers (Australia) Pty Ltd
Sydney • Auckland • London • Cape Town

www.newholland.com.au
www.nhpublishers.com
www.newhollandpublishers.com

1/66 Gibbes Street, Chatswood NSW 2067 Australia
218 Lake Road Northcote Auckland New Zealand
86 Edgware Road London W2 2EA United Kingdom
80 McKenzie Street Cape Town 8001 South Africa

A record of this book is held by the National Library of Australia

ISBN 9781741109092

Publisher: Fiona Schultz
Publishing Manager: Lliane Clarke
Cover Design: Hayley Norman
Production Manager: Olga Dementiev
2D to 3D Stereo Conversion: Inition (Australia) Pty. Ltd.
Lead Stereographer: Markus Stone
Printer: SNP/Leefung Printing Co. Ltd (China)

1 2 3 4 5 6 7 8 9 10